THE
Archive Photographs
SERIES

BINGLEY

The Bingley Coat of Arms.

THE
Archive Photographs
SERIES

BINGLEY

Compiled by
Heather Baldwin and Helen Mills

CHALFORD

The Chalford Publishing Company
St Mary's Mill, Chalford,
Stroud, Gloucestershire, GL6 8NX

ISBN 0 7524 0311 7

Typesetting and origination by
The Chalford Publishing Company
Printed in Great Britain by
Redwood Books, Trowbridge

Bingley - the Throstle's Nest of Old England. A stone plaque at the foot of the riverside steps was sculpted after an idea suggested by Ernest Davies for the opening of the new riverside walk in June 1994.

Contents

Introduction 7

Acknowledgements 8

1. Local Views 9

2. Transport 29

3. Waterways 39

4. Buildings and Monuments 47

5. Young People 61

6. Work and Leisure 75

7. War and Peace 97

8. Around the Villages 107

Main Street, Bingley c. 1900.

Main Street and Chapel Lane c. 1900.

Introduction

Did someone say that Bingley's dead?
  Did someone say it's dying?
It's changed a lot our Throstle's Nest
  Of that there's no denying.
So wander through the town with us
  In photos of the past
And see yesterdays again
  For these are things that last.

Remember when the little shops
  Were all about the town
Remember picture palaces
  Before they all came down
And don't forget the people who
  Were part of long ago
Some of them are strangers
  But many you will know.

We'll stroll along the riverside
  With ancient wells to see
We'll hear the rumble of the looms
  In mills that used to be
And as the shuttles wove the thread
  To keep the pattern bright
A vision and a memory
  Will bring it back to light.

H. Baldwin

Acknowledgements

To all those who kindly loaned photographs for inclusion in the book: H. Baker, H. Baldwin, M. Barnard, F. and H. Bartle, F. Bilborough, L. Butterfield, G. Chew, D. Conchar, M. Davies, J. and E. Earnshaw, C. Firth and family, H. Foster (Courtesy of J.W. Holroyd), A.B. and N. Longbottom, H. Mills, J. O'Melia, A. Pickles, H. Raistrick, R. Reed, M. Robinson, J. Sutcliffe, M. Sutcliffe, B. and J. Thompson, A. Townsend, W. Turnpenny, K. Wagstaff, *Keighley News*, *Telegraph & Argus*, *Yorkshire Post*.

We are greatly indebted to many friends, relatives and acquaintances for the loan of photographs from which we have selected this fascinating collection. In compiling the book we have been priviledged to borrow from treasured family albums and we thank everyone concerned.

Thanks also to Matthew Barnard for his advice and assistance with the layout. Our apologies for any errors or omissions.

Finally, special thanks to Matthew Young of The Chalford Publishing Company for all his help and encouragement.

H. Mills and H. Baldwin
for the Bingley Local History Society, August 1995.

One
Local Views

A view towards the oldest part of Bingley with the White Horse Inn on the left and Old Main Street leading to the Parish Church.

TLE. PARK. LODGE.   BINLEY.

The lodge at Myrtle Grove. This was situated at the foot of the hill approaching the park. When it was demolished the gate posts were moved to their present position at the park entrance.

One of the arches erected in Bingley to celebrate the Jubilee of Queen Victoria in 1887. This one stretched across the top of the town looking down Bradford Road to Peel Mills.

Another arch. This one spanned the Main Street near Chapel Lane. The Old Kings Head can be seen on the right with Dr Lockhead's home and surgery beyond.

Freres Cinema Ltd which later became the Bingley Billiard Hall. Despite thorough investigation the exact site of this building has never been verified.

The relieving office once situated near the Strand.

Regent Street looking toward Airedale Mill. Higher up the street, nearer the Main Road, were rooms used for meetings before the advent of the Mechanics Institute.

The Cartwright family outside their home in Ireland Street opposite the Brown Cow Inn.

These balconies were further down Ireland Street nearer the Gas Works.

Main Street c. 1960. Harrison's Printers, at the end of Regent and Queen Street, were early printers of the Bingley Guardian.

A view from behind the Strand overlooking the River Aire. The house was built in 1852 for the corn merchant Abraham England on the marriage to Martha Binns. Later, this was the offices and workrooms of Thos. Hemmant Grocer.

Commercial Street behind the Queens Head was the site for the stables of Tetley Brewers. Near this roadway was the original "Treacle Alley" believed to have been so named when goods (treacle) were transported from the canal to Slicers mineral works nearby.

Small children playing in the Main Street near Ireland Bridge at the turn of the century. The houses on the right were demolished when the present Main Road was built through the churchyard in 1904.

The Bingley Industrial Co-operative Society, Ltd.,

ESTABLISHED IN 1850

by a few working men for the supply of Food, Clothing and Household Requisites, to be acquired as near the producer as possible.

Profits are divided in proportion to amount purchased.

A struggle for existence marked its early career, but by the pluck and self-denial of its members its troubles were eventually overcome and developed into a fairly vigorous Society. In the present year, 1904, its members number over 3000 or nearly one in five of the population of the district it serves, representing probably over 90 per cent. of the heads of families. Its usefulness may be gauged by the fact that for the last few years trade has averaged over £80,000 annually, and the net profits over £12,000 yearly.

Its **Grocery Stores** are planted all over the town and district.. **Butchering Store** in Chapel Lane with numerous branches. **Drapery, Outfitting, Shoes, and Furniture Stores** in Main Street ; in the upper rooms of the same buildings are situate the Offices, Board, and Meeting Rooms.

Confectionery and Tea-rooms, Foundry Hill, close to Station where Tea can be served, fresh brewed, in a few minutes after ordering.

Its Lending Department enables working men to acquire their own dwellings on easy terms of repayment. Entrance fee 6d. Shares can be held from £2 to £200, and loans to a larger amount. The Society is a convenient and safe repository of the savings of its members, the funds being protected by ample reserves. All will find their connection with the Society an advantage.

☞ **COME AND JOIN.**

WM. HARTLEY, Secretary.

An advertisement for the Co-op.

J. STEPHENSON

Chapel Lane & Main Street.

Stephenson's shop at the corner of Chapel Lane and Main Street c. 1898.

The last of Myrtle Place being pulled down in April 1973. The six tall windows were the living quarters of J. Perfect, chemist, who in 1873 -amongst other wares- advertised to "extract teeth carefully"!

On a cold wet day in May 1953 Bingley people turned out to watch the procession along the Main Street marking the Coronation of Queen Elizabeth II.

The Hebble Bus Terminal in 1958. In front of the terminal were the public toilets better known as "Tom Snowden's Folly". (Copyright *Keighley News*).

Myrtle Place looking to Myrtle Farm which was demolished, along with the houses on the right, to make way for the Bingley Health Centre.

Another view of Myrtle Place with Chapel Lane in the distance across the Main Road. Mrs Pitchforth's hairdressers is on the left next to James Hardaker Art Studio.

H.R.H. Princess Mary with her husband the Earl of Harewood opening the Princess Hall in November 1927.

Leonard Street c. 1969. Emsley Street, Horsfall Street and Hulbert Street are in the process of being demolished.

North Street Post Office, on the corner of Church Street and North Street, just before demolition. The proprietor was Mr Harry Gill and his assistant, seen here with the dog, was Miss Lilian Ogden.

The Seven Dials end of Chapel Lane included The Fashion House, Bilborough's Newsagents, Wilkinson's Confectioners, Spencer and Hill and Ben Ingham's furniture store. After demolition the site became the Midland Hill car park.

The other side of Chapel Lane showing the Co-op butchers, Newall's shoe shop and further along Miss Healey's haberdashery.

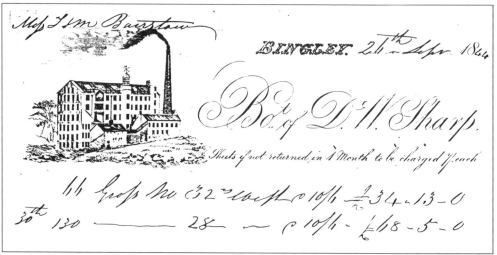

An 1844 invoice sent out to the customers of D.W. Sharp of Prospect Mills.

Prospect Mills, as seen from Chapel Lane, now the site of the shopping precinct.

Old Main Street. On the right is the Grammar Schoolmaster's house which, for a short time, was the home of author Halliwell Sutcliffe. In the background is the Ring of Bells public house.

This building, erected in Myrtle Park in 1951, was used as a Nursery School, a clinic and an old folks centre before being demolished to make way for the Building Society.

The Loft Cafe in Main Street was a popular meeting place for ladies of the town.

Another popular spot on the Main Street, near the library, was the Central Cafe. Miss Lucy Longbottom is pictured here serving on the last days of the shop in 1968. (Courtesy of the *Bradford Telegraph & Argus*).

Many a tale was told when the veterans met at the shelter at the top of Hulbert Hill on the corner of Park Road and Priestthorpe. This was provided by Mr Jonas Hanson in 1935. (Copyright *Keighley News*).

A glimpse of Park Road before the canal was moved in preparation for the future Bingley by-pass.

Mornington Road Methodist Church, pictured from Charles Street, is an unmistakable landmark. Built in 1874, this spacious building, with its 160 foot spire, owed a great deal to the generosity of Alfred and William Sharp.

Two
Transport

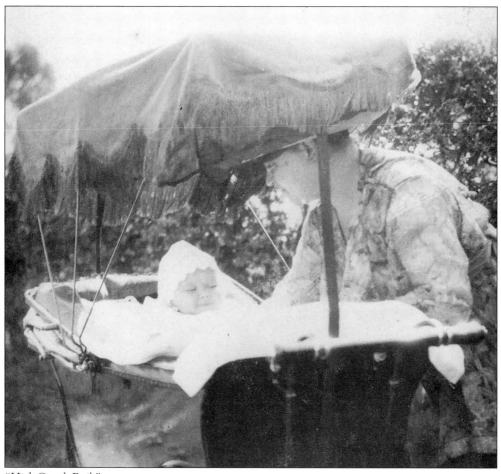

"High Coach Built".

A picture of the first running of the No.96 tram to Bingley seen here at the end of Ann Street and opposite the site of the present police station.

A busy day in Main Street in the 1930's - but not as busy as today !

An old fire engine being towed along the Main Street. In the distance are the Hippodrome and the Old Queens Head Inn.

The Keighley bound platform at the old railway station. Note the Parish Church tower in the background.

The Bradford bound platform on the day before the station was moved to its present position in 1892.

Outside the new station. Note the hut which was once used as a cab drivers shelter.

L.M.S. "Claughton" (Class 4-6-0, No. 5932) approaches Wagon Lane Bridge in 1940. In the background is Holy Trinity Church.

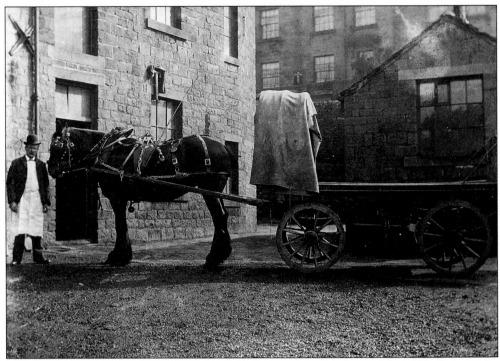

A Co-op horse and cart on its daily round near the gas works while a small child looks over the railings along Ireland Street.

A horse and cart being driven up Harden Road at the end of Altar Lane. Behind is "*Hells Kitchen*" (near to the "*Brown Cow*") which was used as an entertainments centre for billeted servicemen during the Second World War.

John and Edith Whitwham, with Edith Sunderland, amongst fellow travellers setting off from Bingley for Keswick. Note the speed !

The first tram into Bingley on 3rd February 1914. Councillor Tom Snowden, Chairman of B.U.D.C., is centre on the upper deck.

BINGLEY URBAN DISTRICT COUNCIL.

Public Health Department.

SMALLPOX.

Smallpox is spreading in the neighbourhood. It is within the power of everyone to escape the disease by means of vaccination, which will be done free of cost on application to the Public Vaccinator, Dr. J. M. Crocker, Main Street, Bingley.

Be vaccinated and so protect yourself and help to protect the public.

H. ANGUS, M.D.,

Medical Officer of Health.

Dr Meadmore Crocker and his family setting off from their home Albion House on Main Street c. 1930.

Miss M. Tomlinson with her pony and cart in Trinity Place.

A cyclist pauses to enjoy the scenery at the Cottingley Bridge end of Beckfoot Lane.

George Mills shows off his new "*sit up and beg*" bike in Unity Street c. 1934. The uneven sets of the street must have made for a bumpy ride!

Three
Waterways

A view toward the river bank taken from Ferrand Lane, toward the Queen's Court 'Landings' and leading to Watering Well hill with Sharp's Mill above.

The river flowing past the weir towards Ireland Bridge and Hempels Fat Refiners (now replaced by a modern housing estate).

An old corner of Hempels near the bridge.

Boating on the river - a popular pastime in the early years of this century.

Beckfoot Bridge, which crosses Harden Beck, was built in 1723. The farm behind, partly rebuilt in 1617, had Knights Templar connections, indicated by the stone lanterns.

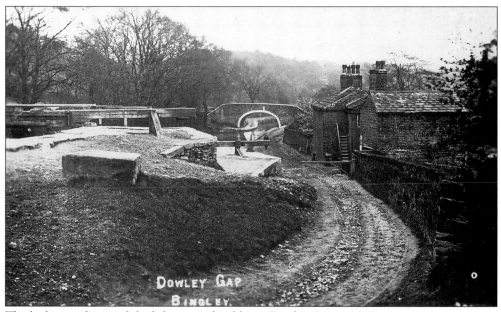

The lock over the canal, lock-house and stables at Dowley Gap c. 1920.

The Leeds and Liverpool Canal two hundred year celebrations. Councillor Raistrick, Chairman of the Committee, opens the proceedings on 23rd March 1974.

Firing the salute at the top of the '5 Rise'.

A crowd gathered at the 5 Rise Lock for the celebrations.

Various pleasure craft moored along the bank at Crossflatts.

A 'traffic jam' on the canal, September 1976.

A view from the 'tin bridge' across the canal into the heart of industrial Bingley. The railway station can be seen beyond the crane.

44

The iron bridge spanning the river from Myrtle Park towards the allotments and Beckfoot Lane.

A modern view of Watering Well Hill behind the former Airedale Street. The owners of Airedale (Sharps) Mill used a donkey engine to pump water from the river to Prospect Mills in Chapel Lane.

This plaque, seen here near Ailsa's Well, was dedicated in 1994 to the memory of Ernest Davies, who together with the 'Better Bingley' campaign, worked so hard to beautify this stretch of the river.

Remembering ERNEST DAVIES *who loved* BINGLEY *and tried to make it a* PLEASANTER PLACE

Ernest Davies, local historian, conservationist and former valued committee member of the Local History Society.

Four
Buildings and Monuments

Bingley Parish Church in 1895 as photographed by George Whitaker.

The Old Vicarage in Park Road c. 1900. After the sixteenth century the property belonged to the Dobson family. The nearby Tithe Barn was demolished in 1910.

The Parish Church Vicarage across the Main Road from the Parish Church was built in 1840. (Since the sixteenth century there was no officially recognised Vicarage.) It was abandoned in 1934 - a victim of the Bingley Bog - when the rectory on Hall Bank Drive was bought.

Bingley Grammar School, another victim of the bog, was built in 1853 (although its history goes back to 1529). Ten years later it was transferred to its present site across the main road towards Castlefields.

Bingley Training College for Ladies opened in 1911 on the site of Lady House Farm after fierce competition between Bingley, Haworth, Otley and Shipley. The college closed in 1980.

Gawthorpe Hall with a history going back to the fifthteenth century. Gawthorpe is said to be haunted by the Grey Lady - a nun believed to have been murdered by her lover! A secret tunnel, arched with oak beams, ran from the Hall to the Parish Church.

Ravenroyd, on the banks of the river Aire near Marley, was a home to prominent Quakers. Records show that in 1378 an Adam Ravenroid paid a poll tax of 4d.

Ashfield House was home to the Sharp family. Many streets off Mornington Road are named after members of the family.

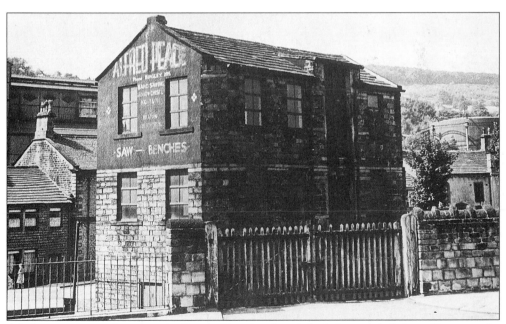

A light engineering firm near the Parish Church - demolished along with Belman Row to make way for the Garden of Rememberance on the eastern side of the church.

St. Ives Mansion, once the home of the Ferrands, was originally Harden Grange. Built on land generated by the monks of Rievaulx Abbey in the thirteenth century it became St. Ives in 1854 and was eventually bought by the council in 1928 for £39,500.

The Gothic Screen at St. Ives denoted ownership by the crusading orders of military monks, the Knights Hospitallers and Knights Templars.

The obelisk above St. Ives is a memorial to W. Busfeild Ferrand M.P. He worked tirelessly to improve the condition of child labour until his death in 1889.

Lady Blantyre's Rock, just below the obelisk. This was a favourite spot for Lady Blantyre who was the mother-in-law to W.B. Ferrand. She passed away in 1896.

Ryshworth Hall at Crossflatts: an ancient house which was renovated and added to many times. The Eltoft family sold it to Edward and Abraham Bynnes in 1591 and in 1672 it became the property of the Busfeild family.

A carving recently uncovered just inside the main entrance to the house.

A modern view of the Market Hall, Buttercross and stocks in tranquil surroundings in the Prince of Wales Park. The stocks stood in Main Street until 1888 when they were moved up to the Park and then more recently re-erected near the Arts Centre.

St. Davids Ruin, a folly built in woods in 1796 by Benjamin Ferrand. The land is now privately owned and known locally as 'Pake Woods' above Harden Grange.

The Crown Inn at top 'o' town near the junction of Ann and James Streets, was opened in the 1860s.

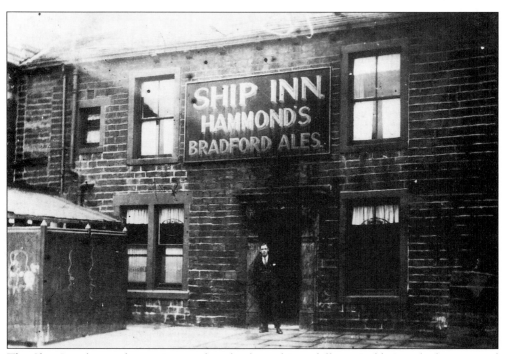

The Ship Inn, licensed in 1862, stood at the foot of Ferncliffe on Dubb Row looking toward Eldon Place.

The Brown Cow Inn near Ireland Bridge. Here the trustees of the Turnpike Trust used to meet, including J.A. Busfeild, Benjamin Ferrand and Dr. Hartley, the vicar of Bingley. Some years later Mr Charles Hogg set up a private school in an upstairs room.

All Saints Parish Church House, Bingley. Opened May 4th. 1929.

The Ring of Bells Inn on old Main Street was bought for the use of the church by the Weatherheads of Gawthorpe in 1929. It is today the venue for many local society meetings including the Local History Society.

The Granby Inn on Dubb Lane. Gotts' sweet shop is on the left and Newhall and Earnshaws' Mill is beyond. Can the ghost of a child be seen here; perhaps he has come back to play with friends ?

A recent view of the Granby Inn with Ferrand Street on the left. This part of Bingley, like so many, is under threat from the by-pass.

The 'Broad Steps' at the end of North Street down into Eldon Place.

The Co-op slaughter house on Dubb Lane. As children we would lean over the wall, hear the squealing of pigs, a loud crack and then silence...

Cottingley Bridge over the River Aire. The building on the right was a bakery and confectioners owned by Miss Pemberton.

Cottingley Bridge at night, lit only by incandescent gas lighting, during the blackout.

Five

Young People

Jack and Lucy Longbottom with their dog Paddy. A typical studio portrait of the time.

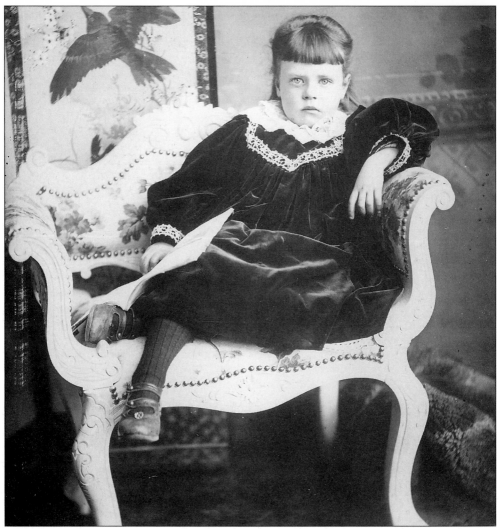

Sarah Alice Moore in her new velvet dress c. 1898. Perhaps her shoes were made by Mr J. Thompson?

A advertisement for Thompsons.

Standard Four boys of the Mornington Road School c. 1906. Pictured centre at the back is Raymond Bailey; Harry Wadsworth is in the striped jersey; George Slicer is the second left on the second row.

The Bingley Grammar School celebrated its 400th anniversary in 1929. The boys are seen here with the headmaster Mr A. Smailes and the Very Right Revd W. Temple D.D., Archbishop of York.

Mornington Road School c. 1920. Those identified are Arthur Longbottom, Jim Heaton, Alan Rushton, Joe Roper, Ernest Seaton, Billy Gott, Lloyd Sadler.

Boys of Mornington Road School practice their drill c. 1915.

A School picture. Back row, left to right: Harry Downs, Albert Jefferies, George Duxbury, Stanley Maude, Henry Hird, Sidney Binns, Eric Feather. Second row: Bill Beckwith, Stanley Johnson, Gordon - , Alan Pickles, Tom Booth, Eric - , Billy Butterworth, Billy Anderson. Third row: Tom Balmforth, Jack Walker, Clifford Denby, Tom Anderson, Kathleen Shaw, Elsie Leach, Florence Roper, Mary Lancaster. Fourth row: Stella Shaw, Tom Speak, Gladys Frear, Ada Winkley, Lulu Rich, Jean Anderton, Hannah Sunderland, -?- , Alice Gallagher, Hilda Heaton. Front row: Mary Robinson, Eric Greenwood, Annie Thornton, Joan Rich, Mary Burley, Gladys Robinson, Norman Wilkinson, Gilbert Walbank. The teacher is Leonard Heys.

What was the theme of this exercise ?!

Children from Holy Trinity dancing round the Maypole c. 1930. Standing, left to right: Evelyn Roper, Betty Barran, Evelyn Knowles, Violet May, Pat Robinson, Evelyn - , Marjorie Baines. Kneeling: Mary Hargreaves, Kathleen King, Mary Barran, Joan Scott, Mollie Walker.

Holy Trinity brownies c. 1930. The Brown Owl was Miss Edith Walker and her assistant Tawny Owl was Mrs Millicent Markham.

Dancing through the ages at Myrtle Park School. Back row, left to right: D. Beck, -?- , P. Longbottom, Joan - , D. Smith, A. Whiteoak, C. Mumby, M. Walker, D. Wilkinson, J. Hall, -?- , G. Rossiter, B. Binns. Front row: G. Lilley, -?- , -?- , I. Roe, P. Sinkinson, E. Swain, V. Cooper, I. Allan, G. Clewes.

Myrtle Park School 1935. The dancing girls are H. Mills, K. Gill, -?- , -?- , M. Pickard, -?- , M. Falkingham

Bingley Parish Church brownies c. 1930. Left to right: Jean Sunderland, Myra Tetley, Winnie Mills, - Wilkinson, Doris Pickles, Dorothy Nichols, Margaret Rowley, Elsie Pickles, Helen Mills, Sarah Stackhouse, Margaret Brakes.

The same group of brownies with the leaders Kitty Smith, May Pickles, Betty and Gertrude Garrard.

Children in class at the Holy Trinity day school c. 1934.

Bingley Parish Church concert at the Princess Hall c. 1934. Back row, left to right: E. McGuire (Bellman), D. Parker, E. Taylor, S. Grunwell, M. Bailey, H. Pickles, D. Goulson, D. Eustace, E. Pickles, M. Ellison, M. Grunwell, M. Brakes, -?- . Front row: M. Eustace, -?- , H. Mills, J. Gascoigne, M. Newton, -?- , N. Leake. The children at the back are B. Leach, C. Emmott, W. Taylor.

Young people from Holy Trinity with their winning tableau from the Bingley Gala of 1931. Left to right: -?- , Eric Vanham, Ellen Hartley, Margaret Falkland, Mildred Taylor, Harold Sutcliffe, Daisy May.

The girls of Carrie Pickles dance class presented a version of Cinderella in 1934. Amongst the cast were Agnes Porter (groom), Carrie Pickles (bride), Dorothy Pickles, Peggy Blythe, Violet Cheyne, Doris Butterworth, Mabel Kenyon, Mary Heaton, Jenny Fryer, Joan Whatmuff, Muriel Jennings, Martha Stephenson, Elsie Hustwick, Margaret Sunderland, Molly Porter.

Bingley Gymnastic Club display some of their well-earned trophies at Myrtle Park School in 1938. Those identified are D. Butterworth, M. Kenyon, H. Mills, A. Bentley, N. Duxbury, L. Berry, L. Cheyne, J. Whatmuff, C. Pickles (coach), M. Heaton, P. Ellis, M. Brakes, M. Spurr, L. Toes, M. Sunderland, M. Smith.

Mothers and toddlers outside the clinic, then held at the Princess Hall, c. 1935.

Holy Trinity Sunday School setting out on their annual trip in 1945.

72

The Chief Scout, Lord Rowallen, at the White Rose Rally, held in Myrtle Park, September 1947. (Coutesy of the *Yorkshire Post*)

Mr and Mrs Escritt presented the trophies at the Bingley Swimming Club in 1956. This group includes Christine Martin, Pat Roper, Mary Heaton, Kathryn Mitchell, Christine Appleyard, Pat Barwick, Ann Crossley, Audrey Haigh.

Lindsay and Joy Winup with their winning springer spaniels, Spot and Dainty, at the 1967 Bingley Show.

Six
Work and Leisure

Bingley Commissioners fire engine and crew ready for duty.

The old Longbottom smithy opposite the Strand in Main Street was demolished in 1913 to make way for the first picture palace named the 'Hippodrome'.

George, Fred and Bert Longbottom with employees outside the smithy . It was rented for £12 per year from Mr Ferrand, to be paid annually at the Brown Cow when a free meal was provided.

Blacksmiths at work with forge and anvil c. 1900.

Outside R. Bentley's, painter and decorator. Miss Pauline Walker is in the background. This picture was taken at their premises which were at the rear of Mushroom Hall in Park Road.

Christmas celebrations for employees at Bingley Mills in 1935. Among the party-goers are M. Campbell, K. Hyde, F. Marshall, H. McQuillan, M. Stephenson, A. Kirkbride, B. Campbell, A. Hird, E. Marshall, K. McQuillan, E. Wilkinson, H. Severn.

Carpet weavers in Bingley c. 1860.

Workers of W.R. & R. Atkinson, Joiners.

Anderton Springs workers, Christmas 1950. Left to right: - Barry, Colin Hey, Sam Johnson, Sam Excell, Mary Logan, George Winup, Phyllis Jones, Eric Clewes.

Menders at a farewell party at the Lilycroft Mills for Miss Beatrice Wilson, seen here being presented with a bouquet by manageress Miss Linda Breadmore. Back row, left to right: H. Mills, N. Hellens, -?- , V. Ibbotson, D. Anderson, M. Hudson, A. Bennett, - Robinson, J. Crabtree. Middle row: A. Gott, M. Wells, D. Toon, K. Nunns, Mrs Farley, P. Dixon, E. Reynolds, E. Hare. Front row: M. Millward, F. Woodcock, -?- , B. Brown, M. Roberts, M. Coulton, - Wingate. (Copyright Keighley News).

Eli Butterfield as a young man. A well known Bingley character, his fishmongers shop was in Chapel Lane.

A one man band who used to entertain the children around the streets of Bingley and the area in the 1930s.

A source of attraction for children, this water fountain used to stand at the Beech Street entrance to Myrtle Park. Here, in about 1935, is Dorothy Mills playing with one of the metal drinking cups.

Bingley Show in the early years. It was first held in Myrtle Park in 1869 but had previously been held in a field near Gawthorpe.

The Walker family in Prince of Wales park. They were Richard, Mary, Pauline, Jessie, Amy, Alice and 'Sis'.

The opening match at the new bowling green in Myrtle Park, 27th May 1906. Johnnie Walker is third left; Seth Parrot is wearing the light trilby; John Barron of Claremont is wearing the straw hat.

Holy Trinity football team c. 1920. Back row, left to right: G. Frankland, J. Weatherhead, E. Tetley, C. Wood, W. Roberts, H. Rhodes, J. Harrison, E. Rumfitt. Middle row: J. Foulds, J. Sharpe, W. Harrison, G. Collier, E. Grunwell. Front row: L. Grunwell, J. Vanham, G. Askey.

Bingley Girls Grammar School first XI, 1909-1910.

W.P.C. Joyce Ascough, a member of the
Bingley Police Force c. 1955.

The carnival King and Queen passing Dracup and Foulds in Myrtle Park c. 1930. Fred Rayner is dressed as the Queen.

FRED RAYNER, The Yorkshire Commedian.

The Yorkshire comedian Fred Rayner and his entertainer son who lived in Leonards Place.

The 'Lady' Fred being helped from 'her' car to attend a civic function.

Mr Robert (Bob) Culbert, a well known Bingley tenor in his role of Lorenzo with co-artiste Mr Pat Lovell.

Rest and relaxation for the W.E.A. hikers as they pause on the moors above Bingley in 1936. Left to right: J. Hall, G. Mills, E. Mills, C. Emmott, C. Burnley, -?- , C. Smith, -?- .

The Ladies of Bingley Independent Methodist Chapel at their connexional conference, June 1929. The minister (second left, front row) is Mrs Wilkinson.

Bingley Parish Church garden party in July 1932. The girls from the Friendly Society show off their flower arrangements. Those identified so far are W. Markham, E. Mills, M. Stevenson, A. Greenwood, N. Cartwright, M. Perfect.

W.E.A. Bingley branch coach trip c. 1936. Back row, left to right: J. L. Whitwham, G. Luscombe, W. Mills, C. Reed, -?- , -?- , - Davies. Front row: F. Newbould, -?- , C. Smith, -?- , Elsie Lee (and child), Edith Whitwham, Alan Keighley.

Bingley Chamber of Trade outing to Morecambe 24th August 1948. There will be quite a few familiar faces including Mr 'Tick-Tock' Walker, Mr Dick Greaves, H. Whatmuff, M. Whatmuff, Misses Tomlinson, H. Wilson, M. Ward, John Pickles, W. Foulds.

ELDWICK & GILSTEAD GLEE UNION 1935-6

Eldwick and Gilstead Glee Union 1935. The Union was formed in 1931 and became the Eldwick and Gilstead Male Voice Choir in 1939. Pictured here are Bert Smith, H. Sercombe, Chris Cooper, Maurice Rothery, Feather Spencer, Jim Whiting, Harry Priestley.

A presentation to Councillor Arthur Bentley in 1950. Those identified so far are P. Bond, C. Scott, H. Whitehead and F. Dunhill.

Ladies of Bingley Parish Church Mothers Union with sleeves rolled up to tackle the dirt in the tower. Some of those present were Mrs Townsend, Mrs Mills, Mrs Chadwick, Mrs Tidswell, Mrs Ford and her daughter Maureen, Mrs J. Chadwick, Miss Weeeks, Miss Hilary and the Revd J. Townsend. (Copyright *Keighley News*).

Did time stand still when the Church clock was being repaired during the 1960s.

Bingley Parish Church Youth Fellowship entertaining members of an esperanto group in 1948. (Copyright *Keighley News*).

Bingley Parish Church Mothers Union outside the railway station on their annual outing. Back row, left to right: F. Moore, Mrs Cowbourne, Mrs Tidswell, -?- , Mrs Sharp, Mrs Potter, Mrs Townsend. Front row: Mrs Moore, Miss Wright, Mrs Frampton, Mrs Stead, Mrs Garnett, Mrs Wilkinson, Revd J. Townsend, Mrs Emmott, -?- , Mrs Smith, -?- , Mrs Mills, Mrs Batley.

Mr and Mrs Chapman (front) entertained members of the Bingley Mixed Hockey team at Bankfield Hotel in 1959. The members include Alfred Butler, Ronnie Summers, Lily Green, Walter Chapman, Tom Lawson, Fred Wildman, Frank Moulden, Edna Chapman, Miss Butler, Donald Heron, Norman Green, Ralph Dixon, Mrs Wildman, Ethel Dixon, Elsie Greenwood, Olive Heron, Mrs Moulden, Sally Pearson, Mrs Bower, Sidney Bower.

Helpers at the Old Folks Centre in Myrtle Park gave a concert for members in 1960. Back row, left to right: -?- , Mrs Leach, -?- . Centre: Mrs Cheetham, Mrs Allinson, -?- , -?- , Mrs Mills, Mrs Goldsborough, Mrs Ryecroft, -?- . Front: Mrs Kasapian, Mrs Rushton, -?- , Mrs Garrett, -?- . (Copyright *Keighley News*).

The sheep dog trials, once a very popular event in Bingley, were held in Low Meadow. Mr M. Hayton is in the arena while J. Lee Whitwham and E. White look on.

Enjoying a pint together are Mr Tony Davies, journalist, and Mr John Braine, one of the 'Angry Young Men', author of 'Room at the Top' and a former Bingley Librarian.

Seven

War and Peace

To let you know I'm doing "My Bit"
With the "R.F.A." (in training),
A Regiment with a record
Of Glory, never waning,
And my only one ambition
Is, whatever may befall,
To uphold the reputation
Of my Comrades one and all.

From
one of the
R.F.A.

General Booth, founder of the Salvation Army, addresses a crowd at Myrtle Park in July 1907.

General Rundle of the Royal Artillery at the South African War Memorial Ceremony outside the Mechanics Institute in 1905. On the platform are Mr G.W. Foster (Chairman of the Council), Revd F.W. Bardsley of Holy Trinity, Archdeacon Kilner (Vicar of Bingley), and Mr W. Ferrand. General Rundle served under Lord Kitchener during the Nile and Khartoum expeditions.

Troops of the Royal Artillery forming a guard of honour outside the church in Old Main Street in June 1905.

The Bradford Pals approaching Poplar House on their march from Bradford to Skipton in 1912.

Recruiting Officer Charles May leading soldiers down Park Road to the railway station during the Great War.

The Peace celebrations Saturday 19th July 1919. This tableau depicted the newly formed League of Nations. Represented were Uncle Sam (Mr Walker of the Post Office); France (May Frear); John Bull (Tony Park); Miss League of Nations (Netta Rushton); Sailor Boy (Master Harrison).

Another tableau, this one welcoming babies. The driver is Mr Alf Whiteley.

WAR MEMORIAL, MYRTLE PARK BINGLEY

The dedication of the Cenotaph in Myrtle Park commemorating those who gave their lives in the First World War.

Councillor Penn about to lay a wreath at the Cenotaph on Armistice Day 1959 surrounded by members of the council and public. Those present are B.L. Moulson, A. Haslock, J. Escritt, M. Longbottom, B. Lax, M. Rothery, S. Cross, M. Calvert, M. Barnard (with the wreath), L. Kershaw, H. Waddington, L. Taylor, A. Markham (altar boy).

Special Constables, with Wardens behind, assembling ready to march to a civic Sunday service in 1939.

Councillors on their way to a Sunday service in the Parish Church in 1967. Left to right: Mr Bond, Mr Haslock, Mr Lax, Mr Dunhill, Mr Arnfield, Mr Cowbourne, Mr Scott (with bowler hat), Mr and Mrs J. Stone.

Bingley Naval Association dinner held in the Ambulance Hall in December 1949. The toast 'to our allies' was proposed by Mr A.W. Platts. The response was by Mr N. Lancaster (U.S. Consul in Bradford).

The Association dinner menu with signatures of those present.

Bingley & District Naval Association.

Chairman: *Alfred W. Platts,*
1, *Park Road,*
Bingley.
Tel. Bingley 27 & 2858.

Treasurer: *Stanley Craven,*
9, *Charles Street,*
Bingley.

Secretary: *Harry Frear,*
5, *Cardigan Street,*
Bingley.

<u>MISS N. MILLS.</u>

Cream of Tomato Soup

Roast Turkey

Brussel Sprouts, Turnips & Mashed Potatoes

Christmas Pudding & Rum Sauce

Mince Pies

Cheese & Biscuits

Coffee

TOAST LIST.

"The King".

"The Town & Trade of Bingley" . Proposed by: W. T. Smith Esq.,
Response: John Wild Esq., J.P.,
Chairman of the Bingley U.D.C.

"Our Allies" . Proposed by: A. W. Platts Esq.
Response: N. Lancaster Esq.,
United States Consul in Bradford.

---- Dec 1949.

Children of Bingley Modern School, now Beckfoot Grammar, celebrating V.E. Day in 1945.

Eight
Around the Villages

The Lodge at St. Ives, Cottingley. This stood higher up than the Sun Inn.

Cottingley Bar and the Toll House on the Main Road looking towards Bankfield.

The Sun Inn, better known locally as Nancy's. It has welcomed wayfarers for at least 300 years. The 'snug' of this old coaching inn served as both court house and a rendezvous for poachers.

Cottingley Town Hall opened in 1865 by Lord Frederick Cavendish: its name was originally intended to be Protestant Hall.

The congregation of Cottingley Town Hall c. 1930.

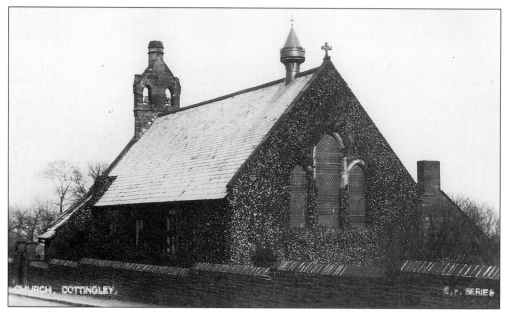

St. Michael and All Angels Church at Cottingley caught fire and was later demolished. The site is now occupied by modern flats.

The interior of St. Michaels.

Mr Sam Neale of Cottingley, with his dogs, after having caught a fox c. 1931.

St. Michaels Sunday school party 1923. The children were entertained with a concert titled 'A *string of Beads*'.

Cottingley Town Hall Ladies after a performance of '*Ahr Jack's Will*' in 1933.

Cottingley Working Men's Club.

Throstle Nest Farm, Cottingley. Mr H. Willis is delivering the milk.

Children enjoy the Punch and Judy show at Cottingley Gala in 1969.

The Lodge at Harden Grange. Note the gateposts on the left which were presumed to be a carriage entrance to St. Ives.

Harden from Malt Shovel.

Ivy House Farm, Harden, was built by Samuel Sunderland in 1676 and later acquired by the Ferrands. The Crowther family have farmed here since 1899.

The present farmer, Mr Joe Crowther, leading one of his bulls out to pasture.

Twins George and Joe Crowther of Ivy House with their trophy, a fox, outside the barn c. 1941.

116

Goit Stock in the early 1920s - owned by Mr Dewhirst and a popular pleasure park near the Malt Shovel, Harden.

The interior of Goit Stock Cafe which was reputed to seat up to 1000 people.

Long Lane, Harden, c. 1900.

Harden Wesleyan Reform Chapel 'At Homes !', was opened by Councillor Ken Eckersley; beside him is Ruth Crowther. Waiting to be served (amongst others) are Mavis Crowther, Mary Pearce, Helen Mills, Joan Coulton, Miss Sant. (Copyright *Keighley News*).

Crossflatts Day School in 1924. The headmaster is Mr T. Whittingham; also pictured is Eric Fox (fourth right, second row).

Flooding at Castlefields with Myers and Robinson's Mill in the foreground. Mr Ilford Fox assess the damage.

Crossflatts Gala in 1952 and a winning tableau by St. Aidans Sunday school. The vicar is John Fox with Philip Atack next to him. On the extreme left is Ruth Fox.

St. Aidans Choir about 1968 with the Revd Bruce Grainger and Dr. J. Freeman of Bradford University.

The Mission Hut in Gilstead with its corrugated iron roof served both the local community and those building the nearby reservoir (hence the familiar name 'Navvies Mission'). Mr Tom Porter used to ring the bell every Sunday morning to call people to worship.

The opening of St. Wilfrids Church, Gilstead on 23rd June 1906. The church was consecrated by the Very Right Revd Boyd Carpenter, Bishop of Ripon; behind him, holding a book, is the Revd F.W. Bardsley, Vicar of Holy Trinity, Bingley.

The bottom of Warren Lane showing a rather different scene.

Eldwick Beck Mill, established as a worsted spinning mill in 1800, was originally powered by a massive water wheel and later by steam. After demolition the stone was carried to the village centre to build Eldwick Memorial Hall which opened in October 1956.

The old chapel at High Eldwick, dated 1815, remained derelict for many years but was formerly a day school. Pupils came from the scattered crofts and farms nearby and attended at a cost of few pence weekly.

Children of High Eldwick Chapel and school c. 1880. Martha Ann Wildman is pictured (second from the left, back row).

The Fleece Inn, High Eldwick, better known as 'Dick Hudsons' after a former landlord who resided in late Victorian times. The licensee here is Mr Richard Garnett.

Julia Wildman with her pet lamb and dog outside High Crag Farm c. 1900.

Arthur Wildman of Eldwick (left) with
Jimmy 'Mouldy Warp' Greenwood
(molecatcher) outside Dick Hudsons c.
1900.

Crag Wood Farm caravan field c. 1911.
Several families came for the summer
holidays or weekends and enjoyed the use of
the communal camp kitchen. The 'caravans'
were old railway carriages. Arthur
Longbottom is in the centre with his sister
Elsie behind and Jesse Wilkinson to the left.

Eldwick Village school in 1927. Back row, left to right: George Baxter, Edgar Greenwood, Donald Wilkinson, Sandy Darling, Herbert Sharp, Jimmy Greenwood. Third row: Stanley Whiting, Phylis Eichel, Rita Sayner, Nancy Whiting, Jack Sharpe, Eileen Todd, -?- , Rennie Greenwood. Second row: Freda Sayner, Edith Holgate, Rita Follett, Grace Whiting, Joan Whiting, Lily Murgatroyd, Jean Varey. Front row: Freddie Clark, - Eichel, -?- , Donald Woolsey, Ralph Eichel.

Eldwick school in 1946. The Headmaster is Mr W.A. Birch; the teachers are Mr L. Cooke and Mrs Birch.

St. Lawrence's Garden party c. 1939. Those identified so far are Revd Canon C. Tremayne, Mrs H. Smith, J. Butterfield, K. Holt, Florrie and Jessie Holmes, Amy Royston, Doris Pickles, Mr Armistead, Mrs and Miss Eichel, Mabel Ashby, Edna Pickles, Martha Longbottom with her grandchildren Rita and Mary, Mrs Edwards, J. Butterfield (Jnr), P. Whiting, J. Edwards.

Another St. Lawrence Garden party c. 1950. Those present include Revd J. Townsend, Mr K. Moss, Mrs Townsend, Mr W. Birch.

'Beating the bounds', Rogationtide May 1950. The choristers include Paul Townsend, Frank Longbottom, Leonard Butterfield, Mary Longbottom, Geoffrey Longbottom, David Wildman, Eric Longbottom, Paul Swinden, Bruce Garside, Stuart Driver, Ann Charlesworth, Joan Blomfield, Rita Longbottom, Mrs Adcock, Mrs McKay, Wendy Adcock, Mrs Townsend, Mrs Morse, Miss Wymark, Meadmore Preston, Fred Adcock, Mr Lockier.

Jack White, huntsman, heads home along Spring Lane, Eldwick c. 1955. The Airedale Beagles were formed in 1890.

Stock List

(Titles are listed according to the pre-1974 county boundaries)

BERKSHIRE

Wantage
Irene Hancock
ISBN 0-7524-0146 7

CARDIGANSHIRE

Aberaeron and Mid Ceredigion
William Howells
ISBN 0-7524-0106-8

CHESHIRE

Ashton-under-Lyne and Mossley
Alice Lock
ISBN 0-7524-0164-5

Around Bebington
Pat O'Brien
ISBN 0-7524-0121-1

Crewe
Brian Edge
ISBN 0-7524-0052-5

Frodsham and Helsby
Frodsham and District Local History Group
ISBN 0-7524-0161-0

Macclesfield Silk
Moira Stevenson and Louanne Collins
ISBN 0-7524-0315 X

Marple
Steve Cliffe
ISBN 0-7524-0316-8

Runcorn
Bert Starkey
ISBN 0-7524-0025-8

Warrington
Janice Hayes
ISBN 0-7524-0040-1

West Kirby to Hoylake
Jim O'Neil
ISBN 0-7524-0024-X

Widnes
Anne Hall and the Widnes Historical Society
ISBN 0-7524-0117-3

CORNWALL

Padstow
Malcolm McCarthy
ISBN 0-7524-0033-9

St Ives Bay
Jonathan Holmes
ISBN 0-7524-0186-6

COUNTY DURHAM

Bishop Auckland
John Land
ISBN 0-7524-0312-5

Around Shildon
Vera Chapman
ISBN 0-7524-0115-7

CUMBERLAND

Carlisle
Dennis Perriam
ISBN 0-7524-0166-1

DERBYSHIRE

Around Alfreton
Alfreton and District Heritage Trust
ISBN 0-7524-0041-X

Barlborough, Clowne, Creswell and Whitwell
Les Yaw
ISBN 0-7524-0031-2

Around Bolsover
Bernard Haigh
ISBN 0-7524-0021-5

Around Derby
Alan Champion and Mark Edworthy
ISBN 0-7524-0020-7

Long Eaton
John Barker
ISBN 0-7524-0110-6

Ripley and Codnor
David Buxton
ISBN 0-7524-0042-8

Shirebrook
Geoff Sadler
ISBN 0-7524-0028-2

Shirebrook: A Second Selection
Geoff Sadler
ISBN 0-7524-0317-6

DEVON

Brixham
Ted Gosling and Lyn Marshall
ISBN 0-7524-0037-1

Around Honiton
Les Berry and Gerald Gosling
ISBN 0-7524-0175-0

Around Newton Abbot
Les Berry and Gerald Gosling
ISBN 0-7524-0027-4

Around Ottery St Mary
Gerald Gosling and Peter Harris
ISBN 0-7524-0030-4

Around Sidmouth
Les Berry and Gerald Gosling
ISBN 0-7524-0137-8

DORSET

Around Uplyme and Lyme Regis
Les Berry and Gerald Gosling
ISBN 0-7524-0044-4

ESSEX

Braintree and Bocking
John and Sandra Adlam and Mark Charlton
ISBN 0-7524-0129-7

Ilford
Ian Dowling and Nick Harris
ISBN 0-7524-0050-9

Ilford: A Second Selection
Ian Dowling and Nick Harris
ISBN 0-7524-0320-6

Saffron Walden
Jean Gumbrell
ISBN 0-7524-0176-9

GLAMORGAN

Around Bridgend
Simon Eckley
ISBN 0-7524-0189-0

Caerphilly
Simon Eckley
ISBN 0-7524-0194-7

Around Kenfig Hill and Pyle
Keith Morgan
ISBN 0-7524-0314-1

The County Borough of Merthyr Tydfil
Carolyn Jacob, Stephen Done and Simon Eckley
ISBN 0-7524-0012-6

Mountain Ash, Penrhiwceiber and Abercynon
Bernard Baldwin and Harry Rogers
ISBN 0-7524-0114-9

Pontypridd
Simon Eckley
ISBN 0-7524-0017-7

Rhondda
Simon Eckley and Emrys Jenkins
ISBN 0-7524-0028-2

Rhondda: A Second Selection
Simon Eckley and Emrys Jenkins
ISBN 0-7524-0308-7

Roath, Splott, and Adamsdown
Roath Local History Society
ISBN 0-7524-0199-8

GLOUCESTERSHIRE

Barnwood, Hucclecote and Brockworth
Alan Sutton
ISBN 0-7524-0000-2

Forest to Severn
Humphrey Phelps
ISBN 0-7524-0008-8

Filton and the Flying Machine
Malcolm Hall
ISBN 0-7524-0171-8

Gloster Aircraft Company
Derek James
ISBN 0-7524-0038-X

The City of Gloucester
Jill Voyce
ISBN 0-7524-0306-0

Around Nailsworth and Minchinhampton from the Conway Collection
Howard Beard
ISBN 0-7524-0048-7

Around Newent
Tim Ward
ISBN 0-7524-0003-7

Stroud: Five Stroud Photographers
Howard Beard, Peter Harris and Wilf Merrett
ISBN 0-7524-0305-2

HAMPSHIRE

Gosport
Ian Edelman
ISBN 0-7524-0300-1

Winchester from the Sollars Collection
John Brimfield
ISBN 0-7524-0173-4

HEREFORDSHIRE

Ross-on-Wye
Tom Rigby and Alan Sutton
ISBN 0-7524-0002-9

HERTFORDSHIRE

Buntingford
Philip Plumb
ISBN 0-7524-0170-X

Hampstead Garden Suburb
Mervyn Miller
ISBN 0-7524-0319-2

Hemel Hempstead
Eve Davis
ISBN 0-7524-0167-X

Letchworth
Mervyn Miller
ISBN 0-7524-0318-4

Welwyn Garden City
Angela Eserin
ISBN 0-7524-0133-5

KENT

Hythe
Joy Melville and Angela Lewis-Johnson
ISBN 0-7524-0169-6

North Thanet Coast
Alan Kay
ISBN 0-7524-0112-2

Shorts Aircraft
Mike Hooks
ISBN 0-7524-0193-9

LANCASHIRE

Lancaster and the Lune Valley
Robert Alston
ISBN 0-7524-0015-0

Morecambe Bay
Robert Alston
ISBN 0-7524-0163-7

Manchester
Peter Stewart
ISBN 0-7524-0103-3

LINCOLNSHIRE

Louth
David Cuppleditch
ISBN 0-7524-0172-6

Stamford
David Gerard
ISBN 0-7524-0309-5

LONDON
(Greater London and Middlesex)

Battersea and Clapham
Patrick Loobey
ISBN 0-7524-0010-X

Canning Town
Howard Bloch and Nick Harris
ISBN 0-7524-0057-6

Chiswick
Carolyn and Peter Hammond
ISBN 0-7524-0001-0

Forest Gate
Nick Harris and Dorcas Sanders
ISBN 0-7524-0049-5

Greenwich
Barbara Ludlow
ISBN 0-7524-0045-2

Highgate and Muswell Hill
Joan Schwitzer and Ken Gay
ISBN 0-7524-0119-X

Islington
Gavin Smith
ISBN 0-7524-0140-8

Lewisham
John Coulter and Barry Olley
ISBN 0-7524-0059-2

Leyton and Leytonstone
Keith Romig and Peter Lawrence
ISBN 0-7524-0158-0

Newham Dockland
Howard Bloch
ISBN 0-7524-0107-6

Norwood
Nicholas Reed
ISBN 0-7524-0147-5

Peckham and Nunhead
John D. Beasley
ISBN 0-7524-0122-X

Piccadilly Circus
David Oxford
ISBN 0-7524-0196-3

Stoke Newington
Gavin Smith
ISBN 0-7524-0159-9

Sydenham and Forest Hill
John Coulter and John Seaman
ISBN 0-7524-0036-3

Wandsworth
Patrick Loobey
ISBN 0-7524-0026-6

Wanstead and Woodford
Ian Dowling and Nick Harris
ISBN 0-7524-0113-0

MONMOUTHSHIRE

Vanished Abergavenny
Frank Olding
ISBN 0-7524-0034-7

Abertillery, Aberbeeg and Llanhilleth
Abertillery and District Museum Society and Simon Eckley
ISBN 0-7524-0134-3

Blaina, Nantyglo and Brynmawr
Trevor Rowson
ISBN 0-7524-0136-X

NORFOLK

North Norfolk
Cliff Richard Temple
ISBN 0-7524-0149-1

NOTTINGHAMSHIRE

Nottingham 1897–1947
Douglas Whitworth
ISBN 0-7524-0157-2

OXFORDSHIRE

Banbury
Tom Rigby
ISBN 0-7524-0013-4

PEMBROKESHIRE

Saundersfoot and Tenby
Ken Daniels
ISBN 0-7524-0192-0

RADNORSHIRE

Llandrindod Wells
Chris Wilson
ISBN 0-7524-0191-2

SHROPSHIRE

Leominster
Eric Turton
ISBN 0-7524-0307-9

Ludlow
David Lloyd
ISBN 0-7524-0155-6

Oswestry
Bernard Mitchell
ISBN 0-7524-0032-0

North Telford: Wellington, Oakengates, and Surrounding Areas
John Powell and Michael A. Vanns
ISBN 0-7524-0124-6

South Telford: Ironbridge Gorge, Madeley, and Dawley
John Powell and Michael A. Vanns
ISBN 0-7524-0125-4

SOMERSET

Bath
Paul De'Ath
ISBN 0-7524-0127-0

Around Yeovil
Robin Ansell and Marion Barnes
ISBN 0-7524-0178-5

STAFFORDSHIRE

Cannock Chase
Sherry Belcher and Mary Mills
ISBN 0-7524-0051-7

Around Cheadle
George Short
ISBN 0-7524-0022-3

The Potteries
Ian Lawley
ISBN 0-7524-0046-0

East Staffordshire
Geoffrey Sowerby and Richard Farman
ISBN 0-7524-0197-1

SUFFOLK

Lowestoft to Southwold
Humphrey Phelps
ISBN 0-7524-0108-4

Walberswick to Felixstowe
Humphrey Phelps
ISBN 0-7524-0109-2

SURREY

Around Camberley
Ken Clarke
ISBN 0-7524-0148-3

Around Cranleigh
Michael Miller
ISBN 0-7524-0143-2

Epsom and Ewell
Richard Essen
ISBN 0-7524-0111-4

Farnham by the Wey
Jean Parratt
ISBN 0-7524-0185-8

Industrious Surrey: Historic Images of the County at Work
Chris Shepheard
ISBN 0-7524-0009-6

Reigate and Redhill
Mary G. Goss
ISBN 0-7524-0179-3

Richmond and Kew
Richard Essen
ISBN 0-7524-0145-9

SUSSEX

Billingshurst
Wendy Lines
ISBN 0-7524-0301-X

WARWICKSHIRE

Central Birmingham 1870–1920
Keith Turner
ISBN 0-7524-0053-3

Old Harborne
Roy Clarke
ISBN 0-7524-0054-1

WILTSHIRE

Malmesbury
Dorothy Barnes
ISBN 0-7524-0177-7

Great Western Swindon
Tim Bryan
ISBN 0-7524-0153-X

Midland and South Western Junction Railway
Mike Barnsley and Brian Bridgeman
ISBN 0-7524-0016-9

WORCESTERSHIRE

Around Malvern
Keith Smith
ISBN 0-7524-0029-0

YORKSHIRE
(EAST RIDING)

Hornsea
G.L. Southwell
ISBN 0-7524-0120-3

YORKSHIRE
(NORTH RIDING)

Northallerton
Vera Chapman
ISBN 0-7524-055-X

Scarborough in the 1970s and 1980s
Richard Percy
ISBN 0-7524-0325-7

YORKSHIRE
(WEST RIDING)

Barnsley
Barnsley Archive Service
ISBN 0-7524-0188-2

Bingley
Bingley and District Local History Society
ISBN 0-7524-0311-7

Bradford
Gary Firth
ISBN 0-7524-0313-3

Castleford
Wakefield Metropolitan District Council
ISBN 0-7524-0047-9

Doncaster
Peter Tuffrey
ISBN 0-7524-0162-9

Harrogate
Malcolm Neesam
ISBN 0-7524-0154-8

Holme Valley
Peter and Iris Bullock
ISBN 0-7524-0139-4

Horsforth
Alan Cockroft and Matthew Young
ISBN 0-7524-0130-0

Knaresborough
Arnold Kellett
ISBN 0-7524-0131-9

Around Leeds
Matthew Young and Dorothy Payne
ISBN 0-7524-0168-8

Penistone
Matthew Young and David Hambleton
ISBN 0-7524-0138-6

**Selby from the William Rawling
Collection**
Matthew Young
ISBN 0-7524-0198-X

Central Sheffield
Martin Olive
ISBN 0-7524-0011-8

Around Stocksbridge
Stocksbridge and District History Society
ISBN 0-7524-0165-3

TRANSPORT

Filton and the Flying Machine
Malcolm Hall
ISBN 0-7524-0171-8

Gloster Aircraft Company
Derek James
ISBN 0-7524-0038-X

Great Western Swindon
Tim Bryan
ISBN 0-7524-0153-X

Midland and South Western Junction Railway
Mike Barnsley and Brian Bridgeman
ISBN 0-7524-0016-9

Shorts Aircraft
Mike Hooks
ISBN 0-7524-0193-9

This stock list shows all titles available in the United Kingdom as at 30 September 1995.

ORDER FORM

The books in this stock list are available from your local bookshop. Alternatively they are available by mail order at a totally inclusive price of £10.00 per copy.

For overseas orders please add the following postage supplement for each copy ordered:
>   European Union £0.36 (this includes the Republic of Ireland)
>   Royal Mail Zone 1 (for example, U.S.A. and Canada) £1.96
>   Royal Mail Zone 2 (for example, Australia and New Zealand) £2.47

Please note that all of these supplements are actual Royal Mail charges with no profit element to the Chalford Publishing Company. Furthermore, as the Air Mail Printed Papers rate applies, we are restricted from enclosing any personal correspondence other than to indicate the senders name.

Payment can be made by cheque, Visa or Mastercard. Please indicate your method of payment on this order form.

If you are not entirely happy with your purchase you may return it within 30 days of receipt for a full refund.

Please send your order to:

> The Chalford Publishing Company,
> St Mary's Mill,
> Chalford,
> Stroud,
> Gloucestershire
> GL6 8NX

This order form should perforate away from the book. However, if you are reluctant to damage the book in any way we are quite happy to accept a photocopy order form or a letter containing the necessary information.

PLEASE WRITE CLEARLY USING BLOCK CAPITALS

Name and address of the person ordering the books listed below:

_____

_____

_____ Post code _____

Please also supply your telephone number in case we have difficulty fully understanding your requirements.   Tel.: _____ - _____

Name and address of where the books are to be despatched to (if different from above):

_____

_____

_____ Post code _____

Please indicate here if you would like to receive future information on books published by the Chalford Publishing Company.
____ Yes, please put me on your mailing list   ____ No, please just send the books ordered below

Title	ISBN	Quantity
....	0-7524-_____-___	_____
....	0-7524-_____-___	_____
....	0-7524-_____-___	_____
....	0-7524-_____-___	_____
....	0-7524-_____-___	_____
	Total number of books	_____

Cost of books delivered in UK = Number of books ordered @ £10 each =£ _____

Overseas postage supplement (if relevant)   =£ _____

TOTAL PAYMENT   =£ _____

Method of Payment   ❏ Cheque   ❏ Visa   ❏ Mastercard   **VISA**

Please make cheques payable to *The Chalford Publishing Company*   MasterCard

Name of Card Holder   _____

Card Number ❏❏❏❏❏❏❏❏❏❏❏❏❏❏❏❏❏❏❏

Expiry date ❏❏ / ❏❏

I authorise payment of £_____ from the above card

Signed _____